Nellie beg

She had arrived in Italy and was well. She was tired and sent greetings to

Nellie handed it to the York. The clerk asked wh had never heard of it!

Nellie barely finished explaining when she heard the ship's bell. She had lost track of time. Her heart beat faster. She looked at her guard. "Can you run?" he asked.

**The most exciting, most inspiring,
most unbelievable stories . . .
are the ones that really happened!**

The $25,000 Flight
Apollo 13
Babe Ruth and the Baseball Curse
Balto and the Great Race
Climbing Everest
The Curse of King Tut's Mummy
Finding the First T. Rex
The Race Around the World
The Titanic *Sinks!*

TOTALLY TRUE adventures!

THE RACE AROUND THE WORLD

How Nellie Bly chased
an impossible dream . . .

by Nancy Castaldo • illustrated by Wesley Lowe

A STEPPING STONE BOOK™

Random House 🏠 New York

For Lucie

Text copyright © 2015 by Nancy Castaldo
Interior illustrations copyright © 2015 by Wesley Lowe

Photograph credits: Cover, pp. 94–97: courtesy of the Library of Congress,
Prints & Photographs Division

Visit us on the Web!
SteppingStonesBooks.com
randomhousekids.com

Educators and librarians, for a variety of teaching tools, visit us at RHTeachersLibrarians.com

Library of Congress Cataloging-in-Publication Data
Castaldo, Nancy F. (Nancy Fusco).
The race around the world / by Nancy Castaldo ; illustrated by Wesley Lowe.
pages cm. — (Totally true adventures)
ISBN 978-0-553-52278-5 (trade) — ISBN 978-0-553-52279-2 (lib. bdg.) —
ISBN 978-0-553-52280-8 (ebook)
1. Bly, Nellie, 1864–1922—Travel—Juvenile literature. 2. Voyages around the world —
Juvenile literature. 3. Women journalists—United States—Biography—Juvenile literature.
I. Lowe, Wesley, illustrator. II. Title.
G440.B67137C37 2015 910.4'1—dc23 2014044976

Printed in the United States of America
10 9 8 7 6 5 4 3 2 1

This book has been officially leveled by using the F&P Text Level Gradient™ Leveling System.

Contents

Chapter One

Technology and travel have changed a lot in the last hundred years. Today we think nothing of calling a friend up to say "I miss you," even if that friend lives in another state or country. We blow out birthday candles in front of a computer so that someone we love can share that special moment over a video chat. Family members fly to see each other for the holidays. But imagine a time when phones and computers didn't exist. Or planes. It was hard to know much about people who lived far away. People outside of Italy might not have known how yummy pizza was. And people in Italy might not have known where New York City was. The world seemed very big.

But the world got a little smaller in the 1800s. It became possible for people to travel around it. Three important things happened. The first transcontinental railroad was finished in 1869. Before then, Americans had traveled west in wagons. Now they could go faster and easier. By 1871, the British connected all of the railways in India. This meant that people and goods could travel easily across India, too. The Suez Canal opened in 1869. Ships could use the canal to sail safely and quickly between Europe and Asia. They didn't have to sail all the way around Africa.

For the first time, anyone could make a plan, buy tickets, and travel the world. The idea was exciting. People did not need to be explorers to see new places. Anyone could go on an adventure.

However, women still faced challenges. There were some rules women needed to follow. It was not common for them to travel alone. Plus, they needed many clothes. Women wore gowns for different days, events, and times of day. They also wore hats and long coats. They carried umbrellas called parasols. It did not make travel easy. All these clothes had to be packed in huge trunks. But a trip around the world was possible.

Jules Verne was one of many people dreaming of such a trip. He was an author. He wrote about amazing journeys. In 1873, he wrote a bestselling book called *Around the World in Eighty Days*. It's about a man named Phileas Fogg who makes a bet with his friends. "I will bet twenty thousand pounds against anyone who wishes that I will make the tour of the world in eighty days or less . . . ," said Phileas Fogg.

Eighty days or less. How on earth could anyone travel from country to country, over seas and land so quickly? Sure, it's possible today to take a trip around the world. You can fly from New York City to London, England, in just under eight hours. But the only way people traveled during the late 1800s was by ship, train, or horse. These took a lot more time. Long delays happened often. Ships could be stuck in harbor for days in bad weather. Trains traveled slower. Horses were even slower than trains.

Still, people wondered: could it be done?

Maybe, by someone smart, tough, and brave. Certainly not by a young woman.

Chapter Two

The woman we know as Nellie Bly was born Elizabeth Jane Cochran. She was nine years old when Jules Verne's *Around the World in Eighty Days* was published. She lived in a tiny town in Pennsylvania. The town was named after her father.

Michael Cochran already had a dozen children when she was born. She was number thirteen. Her mother, Mary Jane, did not dress her like other children in town. They wore dark colors. Instead she wore pink. Pink became her favorite color and her nickname.

Pink's father died when she was just six years old. His death left not only a hole in the family, but also worries over their money. The family's home had to be sold. Pink moved to a smaller home with her mother and the younger children.

Two and a half years later, Pink's mother married again. Things did not go well for the new family. Pink's stepfather had a bad temper. Her mother grew afraid of him. She knew she had to leave with her children. It was a hard choice for a strong woman to make.

Pink was fifteen years old when her mother got a divorce, something very uncommon at the time. Pink had to earn money for the family. She could not think about traveling the world like Phileas Fogg. She decided to become a teacher. Teaching was a respected job for a woman. It would also mean she could take care of herself.

Pink gave up her nickname and became Elizabeth J. Cochrane. She added the "e" to the end of her name because she thought it made it seem more important.

Sadly, money ran out soon after she began, and she needed another plan. She moved to Pittsburgh with her family in 1880. Then, in January 1885, she read something that would change her life.

A reporter had written an article in the *Pittsburgh Dispatch*. It was about how he thought women should act. He felt that women should stay out of the workplace. He wrote that women should turn their attention to cooking, cleaning, and making a nice home. They shouldn't try to be as good as men at anything. It was better to just be helpers.

Elizabeth was outraged. Her mother was a strong woman, so Elizabeth knew that women could not always depend on men. She sent the newspaper a letter. She signed it Lonely Orphan Girl. The editor, George Madden, was so pleased with her writing that he wanted to hear more. He printed a notice in the January 17 issue. He asked

that the Lonely Orphan Girl send her name and address to him.

Elizabeth didn't send her name and address. Instead she went right over to see him. She climbed four flights of stairs to the editor's office. When she arrived, she was out of breath.

But she didn't need to be worried. George Madden was happy to see her. He asked her to write her own article. She went right to work. On January 25, 1885, readers found it in the *Pittsburgh Dispatch.*

THE GIRL PUZZLE
BY LONELY ORPHAN GIRL

Elizabeth wrote about women and work. Women were smart and ready to work, but there weren't many jobs open to them. She wrote that women could do the same jobs as men. Women should also be paid the same as men. George

Madden liked her work. He knew his readers would, too. He asked her to write another article right away.

She wouldn't sign this one Lonely Orphan Girl or Elizabeth Cochrane. She would need another name. Women did not sign their own names to articles at that time. It wasn't proper. It was another rule women had to follow. As her editor rushed her article to press, someone on his staff thought of "Nelly Bly." It was the name of a popular song. Madden liked the name and added it to her article, but he misspelled Nelly. Elizabeth Cochrane now became Nellie Bly.

Nellie wrote many more articles. They were not like the "ladylike" stories by other female reporters. Other women wrote about tea parties and charity events. Nellie wrote about how hard work was for girls in factories. She wrote about jobs that were too dangerous and didn't pay enough.

She went to Mexico as a foreign correspondent. It was her job to let readers in the United States know about things that happened there. She wrote about Mexican bullfights, holidays, soldiers, and politics. Two years later, in 1887, she went to New York City to look for a new job.

It was hard finding one. New York City had several big newspapers. None of them were looking for female reporters. She continued to write and sell stories to the *Dispatch* while she searched.

Nellie became known for her daring stories. They earned her a meeting with the editor at the *New York World,* published by Joseph Pulitzer. The paper gave Nellie a hard assignment. Nellie had to pretend that she was crazy. Then she went to an asylum for the insane. Nobody there knew Nellie was a reporter. Her task was to report on what it was like for the patients. The asylum was supposed to take care of these sick people. She found it horrible. And she wrote about everything she saw when she got out. Nellie had crossed over to a different kind of reporting. She became known as a stunt reporter for putting herself in difficult situations.

Chapter Three

Nellie wrote lots of stories for the *New York World,* but one Sunday night she was stuck for an idea. She tossed and turned in her bed. Every Monday she talked about new stories with her editor. But that night she couldn't think of a single one.

Her editor looked forward to her gutsy ideas. Her readers expected to see her stories in the paper. She had to come up with something. The night was late, and Nellie was tired. She couldn't fall asleep without at least one idea.

I wish I was at the other end of the earth! she thought.

How nice it would be to take a vacation.

Perhaps she *could* travel around the world. Phileas Fogg from *Around the World in Eighty Days* did. What if she traveled around the world, just like him? Why not even faster?

She started planning. She had to find out if it was possible to break Phileas Fogg's record. She looked at steamship timetables. She saw the days and times the ships sailed. It might work. On Monday, her editor asked her if she had an idea. She answered in a timid voice, "One."

He waited for her to tell him what it was.

"I want to go around the world!" she blurted out. She told him that she thought she could beat Phileas Fogg's pace. Could she try it?

His answer was no!

It was the fall of 1888. A woman traveling alone was unheard of. She would need to travel with someone. And even if she could travel alone, how could she take all her trunks of clothing and other important things? Besides, she didn't speak anything but English. No. Only a man could do this.

Nellie was quick with her reply. "Start the man, and I'll start the same day for some other newspaper and beat him."

"I believe you would!" he said. He agreed that if the paper ever sent someone, it would be Nellie. But for now, there would be no trip.

Saddened, she put her grand idea aside. But almost a year later, on November 11, 1889, her editor asked her to come to his office. She went right in and sat in front of him.

He glanced up from his work and asked, "Can you start around the world day after tomorrow?"

Of course she could! She could start that very minute if needed. Her heart began to beat faster. The day after tomorrow? Not much time. But Nellie was intent on bringing her idea to life. Her editor had kept his word.

First she needed to figure out how she would

travel without bringing along lots of clothing. Nellie visited a dressmaker and ordered a dress that she could wear for her entire trip. The dressmaker got right to it. Later that day, he had made a dress of strong blue cloth to last for months of use. Nellie also had a light dress made to wear in the warmer countries. She bought a long, loose coat and one bag about the size of a small backpack.

She brought:
- two traveling caps
- three veils
- a pair of slippers
- handkerchiefs
- needles and thread
- a dressing gown
- a blazer
- underwear
- a small flask and drinking cup
- writing tools—inkstand, pens, pencils, and paper
- gold and paper money

The last thing to fit in the bag was her jar of

cold cream to protect her face from the harsh sea air and sunny weather. After she squeezed everything into the bag, she found she could not fit in her second light gown. It was either the gown or the cold cream. She took the cold cream. She'd manage without the second dress.

The next day, she stepped onto the first of many ships, the *Augusta Victoria*. It would take

her across the Atlantic Ocean to England, her first stop. Friends came to see her off. She wore two watches—one on her wrist that would be set to the local time of each country, and the other tucked in her pocket set to New York time. She kept a gold ring on her left thumb for luck.

Shortly before 9:30 in the morning, the ship's whistle blew. Twenty-five-year-old Nellie tried

to be brave as she watched her friends leave. She had her entire trip ahead of her. Would she be able to beat Phileas Fogg's record?

On Thursday, November 14, 1889, at 9:40 a.m., the ship sailed away from its dock in Hoboken, New Jersey.

Readers of the *New York World* found Nellie's race splashed across the front page.

NOW 30,000 MILES IN A RUSH

Nellie Bly's race around the world had begun.

Chapter Four

As Nellie Bly's journey began, the owner of *Cosmopolitan* magazine was reading about her trip. The owner believed Nellie had made a huge mistake in planning. Nellie was traveling east. He would send their female journalist, Elizabeth Bisland, in the opposite direction to beat Nellie back to New York.

Nellie had no idea that Elizabeth was in a race with her. She was busy getting settled on the ship. The morning was beautiful. Passengers began to get comfy in deck chairs.

"You have now started on your trip," someone said to Nellie. Those words sunk into Nellie like the deep sea. She had never sailed on a ship before, and she began to feel the rocking waves. Nellie moved to the railing of the ship.

"Do you get seasick?" she was asked. Her stomach flipped. She looked down at the waves and threw up over the side.

The watching passengers on deck smiled in sympathy. One man noted, "And she's going around the world!"

Nellie was proud of how bold she was. This was going to be the first of many ships on her trip. Sick or not, she was going to do it!

The captain told her that there was only one way to cure seasickness. She had to force herself to eat. At dinner, when the waiters set a bowl of soup in front of her, she couldn't think of eating it. She held her handkerchief to her mouth and excused herself to the deck. Once she felt a little better, she returned to the table. Each time she felt sick she excused herself to the deck. She returned to the table each time. She was not

going to let the waves get the best of her. The dining guests congratulated her. She had done it! The last course was served. After the meal was finished, Nellie returned to her room on wobbly legs and went to sleep.

When she opened her eyes, she found a stewardess and a female passenger in her room. The captain was standing in her doorway. They were worried. It was 4:30 p.m. Nellie had slept all night and most of the next day. But her seasickness was gone.

Nellie spent the rest of her voyage enjoying the passengers on the ship. One man checked his pulse before and after every meal. Another counted the number of steps he took each day. And there was a family who brought along their dog named Home, Sweet Home. Nellie had a first-class ticket and sailed as a celebrated newswoman. She didn't get to know all the ship's passengers. Many others held steerage-class tickets.

They traveled belowdecks, where it wasn't as fancy.

Back home, the *World* was telling readers that Nellie was halfway across the Atlantic Ocean.

Day after day went by. Finally, land was spotted on the afternoon of November 21. Everyone, including Nellie, rushed on deck to take a look. The rocky bit of bleak coastline looked like paradise after so many days at sea. Southampton,

England, lay ahead. The first leg of her journey around the world was almost done!

But the water was rough. It took much longer to get into the harbor than was expected. The ship didn't arrive until 2:00 a.m. It was a full sixteen hours late! Even more time went by waiting for the tugboat to take the passengers into the

port. Nellie had missed the 1:00 a.m. train she had planned to take to London. She now had to wait for the tugboat to take her to land. Then she could make other plans.

When the gangplank was placed on the tug, a tall, young man greeted Nellie. It was the *World*'s London reporter, Tracey Greaves. Nellie was happy to see him on the tug at that late hour.

There was exciting news. Jules Verne, author of the famous book *Around the World in Eighty Days,* wanted Nellie to visit him. But he lived in France. How on earth could she visit him and not lose more time on her race around the world?

Before she left America, Nellie was given a special passport to go to England. Once there she needed to get a new passport before visiting other countries. She had to travel to London to get it. But she wanted to see Jules Verne, too. Could she do both?

"I think it can be done," said Tracey, "if you are willing to go without sleep and rest for two nights."

They might be able to board a special mail train at 3:00 a.m. if they could clear customs quickly. Nellie's heart beat faster. It was almost three already.

She rushed out into the damp early morning as soon as she finished. Had Nellie missed the train? She strained her eyes to see the tracks through the fog. In the distance she spied the mail train chugging toward the station.

Chapter Five

Nellie and Tracey boarded the only passenger car on the mail train. They sat in a locked compartment. It was heated with a small foot warmer and a smoky oil lamp. They spread newspapers on their laps to catch their crumbs while they ate and chatted. A few hours later, they were in London. Nellie couldn't wait for the porter to unlock their door. She wanted to get going.

While Nellie scurried through London, Elizabeth Bisland arrived in San Francisco. Then she set sail on the *Oceanic* for her first port, Yokohama, Japan. Nellie still had no idea she had a competitor.

There was little time to spare in London before Nellie left for France. Tired and cold, she rode through the fog-filled streets. Castles and towers blurred by her as her horse-drawn cab rushed across the cobblestones. Finally, she arrived at the office of the American Legation.

The American official asked Nellie for her name, address, and birth date. With her new passport in hand, Nellie Bly was ready to make history!

But first she was off to meet the famous author. Jules Verne was waiting for her in France. She climbed back into the carriage to head to the train station. She had just enough time to gobble down a quick breakfast of ham and eggs. Then she and Tracey boarded another train. Tracey asked her to look out the window at the English countryside as the train sped along. Nellie was much too tired.

"What is scenery compared with sleep when one has not seen bed for over twenty-four hours?"

Nellie drifted off to sleep. She didn't wake until the train had stopped. It was time to board another boat. This one would take her across the English Channel to France.

In France, the two had to board another train. She squeezed into a compartment with other passengers. The late-November air sent chills through her. She shared a single foot warmer with everyone else. It was hard not to step on toes. She frowned at the annoyed faces around her.

Nellie was not used to these conditions. The trains in America were much more comfortable. They did not make strangers share tiny locked rooms.

It was late Friday afternoon when the train arrived at Amiens, France. Nellie had barely slept since Wednesday. She worried about how she looked to greet the famous Jules Verne. Tracey yelled for the guard to come and unlock their compartment. They wanted to leave in a hurry.

Jules Verne was waiting on the platform. His wife, Honorine, and Paris journalist Robert Sherard were with him. Their friendly welcome made Nellie forget how messy she felt. The group left in carriages. Nellie rode with Mrs.

Verne. Poor Nellie did not speak French, and Mrs. Verne did not speak English. It made for a quiet ride. Fortunately, it wasn't long. Soon everyone arrived. A large, shaggy black dog greeted Nellie in the courtyard. He jumped up against her and almost knocked her down. Mr. Verne called him away. Nellie liked dogs, but she feared this one would topple her over in front of the famous author. How embarrassing! She was relieved when the dog walked off with his tail drooping.

The group gathered together in a large sitting room.

"Has Mr. Verne ever been to America?" Nellie asked.

Robert Sherard translated the answer into French. Yes, he had, but only once.

"How did you get the idea for your novel *Around the World in Eighty Days*?"

"I got it from a newspaper" was the answer. He had read an article about a trip around the world taking eighty days. He found the idea very

interesting. When he had been younger, he had traveled all over the world on his yacht learning about places. Now that he was older, he did most of his exploring in books.

Nellie went with him to his study. They stood in front of a map of Phileas Fogg's famous journey. Verne had drawn the trip with a blue pencil. Much to Nellie's surprise, Verne took another pencil and drew Nellie's trip beside it.

"If you do it in seventy-nine days, I shall applaud with both hands," he said.

Nellie may have been tired, but she felt wonderful. If only she didn't have another train to catch. Time was moving fast. The Vernes had been so friendly, but she needed to leave.

Honorine Verne kissed Nellie good-bye as if they were old friends. The French couple waved as Nellie and Tracey boarded carriages again.

"Good luck, Nellie Bly," they called.

Chapter Six

The meeting with the Vernes slowed Nellie down, but it also got everyone in the United States talking about her. Tracey wrote an article about the visit. In less than forty-eight hours, it was printed on the *World*'s front page. It even had a drawing of Nellie and the famous author sitting together.

Nellie's adventures didn't just appear in the *World*. Other newspapers picked up the story. Many people were curious about the young American woman traveling with only one dress and one bag. Soon young girls were writing to newspapers, asking about Nellie. How old was she? What did she look like? Nellie was a celebrity.

Nellie arrived in Calais, France, shortly before midnight. Calais was a large, important seaside town. She had two hours to spare before she had to board her train. It would take her to Brindisi, Italy. She decided to walk around the pier. The air was cool and crisp. She saw the Calais lighthouse rising out of the silvery water in the moonlight.

The "India mail train" was famous and expensive. It was made to carry mail from France through Italy. At Brindisi, the mail would be loaded onto ships bound for India and Australia. It was a fast train ride. Passengers needed to

save their places ahead of time. There were only twenty-one private sleeping bunks. They filled up fast. Nellie was happy to get a place in the treasured passenger car.

Nellie thanked Tracey and stepped aboard the train. Once again she was traveling alone. She had not slept much in the last forty-eight hours, so she climbed into her bed and went to sleep. The train rocked and rolled on through the night. When she woke, the car was filled with cigar smoke. Men were playing cards and smoking nearby. She left her bed to wash up in the car's only bathroom. She had a breakfast of bread and coffee. There were many hours ahead before they would reach Brindisi.

In the evening, dinner was served in the dining car. The other women on the train told Nellie that she shouldn't dine with the men. Like the rest of the ladies, Nellie took her dinner back and ate on her bed.

The car was cold at night. Nellie piled every-thing, even her coat, over herself to keep warm. She couldn't see anything out the dirty train win-dows. She went to sleep thinking of the exciting stories she had heard about the passengers who were on the train the week before. Those passen-gers had been lucky. At least they had the excite-ment of getting robbed by bandits on their trip!

The next morning, Nellie pulled open the window shade as the train continued through Italy. *What, no sun?* she thought. She hadn't seen much of England or France. Now the fog was keeping her from seeing Italy.

With nothing else to do, Nellie thought about her trip. She figured out she had sixty-five days ahead of her. She would have to cover about 17,000 miles. That meant she'd have to travel about 262 miles each day. Her stomach fluttered. Was it possible?

The train finally chugged into Brindisi station

at 1:30 in the morning on Monday. It was three and a half hours late. Nellie had only a little over an hour to board her ship, the *Victoria*. This ship would take her to a new continent, Africa.

Nellie caught her breath. She found the *Victoria*, dropped her bag off, and hurried back down the gangplank. She wanted to send a message to the *World*. Did she have enough time? Barely. She went with a guard to the telegraph office. It was a few streets away. When they arrived, Nellie rang for the clerk. She began writing her note. She told the paper that she had arrived in Brindisi and was well. She was tired and sent greetings to her American friends. Nellie handed it to the clerk to send to New York. The clerk asked where New York was. He had never heard of it!

Nellie barely finished explaining when she heard the ship's bell. She had lost track of time. Her heart beat faster. She looked at the guard.

"Can you run?" he asked. She nodded, took the guard's hand, and ran through the Italian streets. When they reached the dock, she breathed a sigh of relief. A ship called the *Alexandria* was sailing

away. Her ship, the *Victoria,* was still there. It was November 25, 1889, eleven days into her journey. Before she knew it she would again be looking out over open water. Her next stop would be in Egypt.

She woke the next morning to find her cabin all wet. She had been splashed with water from her open porthole window. She had no change

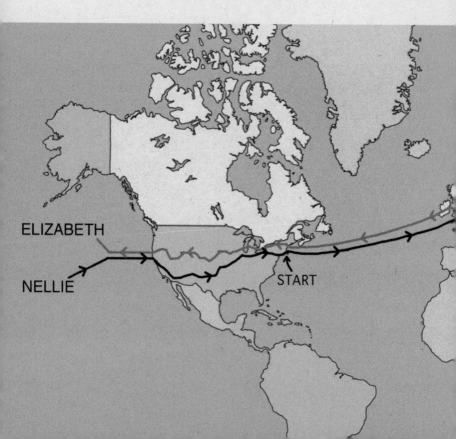

of clothes, but she dried herself off the best she could and went back to sleep.

Nellie was sailing across the Mediterranean Sea. On the other side of the world, Elizabeth Bisland was getting closer to her first stop in Japan.

For both women, there were many more miles ahead.

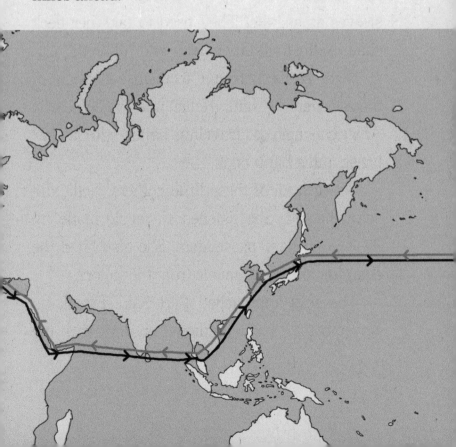

Chapter Seven

Nellie did not enjoy her fellow passengers on the *Victoria*. People brushed her food with their sleeves as she ate. They tried to take her deck chair. Nellie found them rude and "ill-bred."

Nellie seemed strange to them, too. Some of them began to think Nellie was "an eccentric American heiress, traveling about with a hair brush and a bank book."

Between all of these little bothers, Nellie did enjoy herself. She listened to music made by the second-class passengers. She also liked the chanting and drum music from the sailors.

The ship approached Port Said, Egypt, on November 27. Nellie gathered on deck with the other people to watch for the first sight of land. Everyone wanted to step out on shore for a few hours before they sailed again. The ship anchored off shore to load coal. It was used as fuel. Ships came from all over the world to get coal from Egypt.

Small boats sailed out to meet the ship. Nellie and the other passengers climbed down ladders into the small boats. The men took canes with them to keep away beggars. The women took umbrellas. Nellie didn't take anything. She didn't think it was good to hit anybody. She felt that "a stick beats more ugliness into a person than it ever beats out."

When she got to shore, young boys offered rides on burros on the beach. Nellie passed on that. Instead she spent her money on games and shopping. But she only had one bag! What more could she add to it? A sun hat and a scarf!

After a little while, Nellie returned to boats

that would take her back to the *Victoria*. Only this time, the boatmen had a surprise. They doubled the price to take her back to the ship! Nellie had no choice but to pay.

Nellie was not a person who liked to get up early. But the next morning, they would be sailing through the Suez Canal. She did not want to miss that. The Suez Canal was a wonder. It had taken ten years to build. That morning, she rushed up on the deck. But she found the

ship hardly moving. The trip through the canal would take from twenty to twenty-four hours. The canal wasn't as exciting as Nellie had hoped. It looked like a muddy ditch filled with water. There was sandy desert on either side. It wasn't much to look at, but it made her trip around the world possible.

She talked about the canal's history with another passenger during the morning. As the day went on, the sun got higher and hotter.

Nellie sat in her deck chair. Mosquitoes buzzed around her. It might have been unpleasant, but it was much quicker than sailing around Africa!

In the evening, the *Victoria* stopped at Suez. Small sailboats gathered around the large ship. Men from the boats boarded the ship with things for sale. They sold fruit and shells. A magician also came on board. He picked Nellie to help him with a trick.

It was very hot. Nellie changed into a light silk blouse. She was comfortable and "lazily happy." When night came, the men slept on the deck in the fresh night air. The ladies remained belowdecks. They were not allowed back on deck until morning. Nellie would rush up at first light to enjoy the cool air before it grew too hot.

On December 3, the *Victoria* arrived at her next Middle Eastern port—Aden, Arabia. Unlike most passengers, Nellie braved the extreme heat and went ashore. She and a few others took a carriage into town. They rode through a grand stone gate. She saw people selling jewelry, ostrich eggs, shells, and fruit. She watched young boys dive in and out of the ocean for coins. Above them Nellie saw a British flag flying on top of the highest mountain. Nellie had traveled almost 7,000 miles, just a little less than one-third of her trip.

While Nellie was fighting the heat on the *Victoria,* her fame was getting bigger and bigger in America. On November 29, the *World* ran an ad. It announced the "Nellie Bly Guessing Match." How many days, hours, minutes, and seconds would Nellie's trip take? The reader who guessed the closest time would win a first-class trip to Europe.

In less than one week, the *World* had received more than 100,000 guesses. Everyone knew about Nellie's race. And everyone wanted a chance to travel, too.

Chapter Eight

Nellie had left the dry Middle East. Her next stop was Colombo, Ceylon (what we now call Sri Lanka). The lush green island was a happy sight. Palm trees waved in the breeze. It was December 8. Nellie had been traveling twenty-four days. She had less than fifty-six days to beat Fogg's pace.

She had no idea that 100,000 readers were guessing on her trip. She didn't know there was another young woman racing against her. But she knew that with each stop, she was getting closer to the finish.

Nellie rode through the streets. The Grand Oriental Hotel came into view. Its open passages

on the ground floor were the perfect place to sip a cup of Ceylon tea and watch the people walk by. And the jewels! Merchants filled the streets selling shiny emeralds, diamonds, pearls, and rubies.

"No woman who lands at Colombo ever leaves until she adds several rings to her jewel box," claimed Nellie.

Here she was, across the world, on an island paradise. It was a world away from the small Pennsylvania coal town she grew up in. The *World* had written an article ahead of her trip to Ceylon. The newspaper guessed what adventures she might go on. Maybe she would go on an elephant hunt or visit the coffee fields. She might even see beautiful Buddhist temples. Nellie didn't go on an elephant or visit the coffee fields, but she did see temples.

They didn't seem to interest her as much as life on the street. She saw a snake charmer with

a cobra. She also saw small two-wheeled wagons, called rickshaws, for the first time. Men pulled the wagons instead of horses.

One morning, she decided to get up early and take a train to Kandy. Nellie had heard of how beautiful and cool it was. It would be a wonderful day. An hour after she boarded the train, it stopped. She and the other passengers got out of the train and walked to another car for breakfast. Breakfast also brought surprises.

"I thought ... they had prepared a feast for a chicken hawk," wrote Nellie.

She was served fish in vinegar and onions, chicken soup, and chicken every other way she could think of: boiled, fried, cold, and even chicken pot pie! After a full meal, the train continued on. They rode through green valleys planted with rice.

Kandy was not as cool or beautiful as she'd hoped. There were more temples, a library, and a lake. But it was very hot, much hotter than Colombo. After a full day, they returned tired and hot to Colombo.

She was getting anxious to board her next ship, but it had not yet arrived in port. For the first time, she was behind schedule. Her planned two-day stay was growing longer.

The *World* heard from Nellie about the problem. They announced the news.

DECEMBER 12
NELLIE BLY DELAYED!

The clock was ticking. Nellie needed to arrive in Hong Kong on the twenty-eighth. She had to get there on time to board the *Oceanic*. Even a single delay in the coming days would make her miss it. Then she would be too late. She would arrive in New York on February 3—making the trip *eighty-one* days long!

Nellie held her breath.

Chapter Nine

Boarding the *Oriental* did not mean Nellie was on her way again. The ship could not leave until another one had arrived in the harbor. Nellie grew impatient as she stood on the *Oriental*'s deck.

"Colombo is a pleasant place to stay," said one of the passengers.

"It may be, if staying does not mean more than life ...," Nellie answered.

The ship stayed in the harbor for three more days. Finally, at 5:00 a.m. she was called to board. By 9:00 a.m. they were still not moving. Nellie was anxious, and she was hungry.

She ate breakfast in the ship's dining hall

and waited. It was close to 1:00 p.m. when the *Oriental* was ready to sail.

When she was able to leave, she had been away twenty-nine days. She had traveled close to 9,000 miles.

Nellie was running later than ever. But to her surprise, the ship made up time at sea. It quickly sailed across the Bay of Bengal and into the Straits of Malacca!

The weather was hot and sticky. The days aboard were slow and lazy. On December 16, the ship anchored off the island of Penang, now part of Malaysia. It needed to refuel. Six hours on land made Nellie very happy. It gave her a chance to breathe some cool air under the trees. It also gave her time to visit Penang's famous waterfall.

Nellie was less than one hundred miles from the equator. It was the farthest south her journey would take her. Even more important—she was exactly halfway around the world! She had been

away for thirty-three days. She still had to cross the South China Sea against winds, which would make her race even more difficult.

The *Oriental* arrived in Singapore. She was eager to explore another place while the ship refueled. She rode through the streets of Singapore during the day. In the evening, she had dinner with another passenger at the Hotel de l'Europe. There were so many different people in Singapore.

They ate French food served by Chinese waiters. The people all around them were speaking in different languages. Nellie knew she was far from home.

On her way back to the ship, Nellie stopped at the house of her driver. She noticed a macaque monkey standing in their doorway. There were lots of monkeys in Singapore. Merchants sold monkeys, jewels, and other things in the streets.

Up until now Nellie had stopped herself from buying things that might hamper her travel. This monkey was different. It was older than the young ones sold on the street. It looked like it could handle the voyage back to America. She couldn't help herself. She began to bargain for it. When Nellie boarded the ship, she had a small furry friend with her.

It was December 17. Not far away, Elizabeth Bisland was sailing toward Nellie in Singapore. She was also about halfway through her trip around the world. Would they meet? Nellie still had no idea that Elizabeth was even racing her. What if the two ships crossed paths?

The *Oriental* entered the South China Sea and sailed right into a storm. Nellie had not seen anything like the wild sea before. It lifted the boat on its waves and knocked it back down again. Spray covered the decks. The air below was heavy and stuffy. Nellie and her monkey fought seasickness with the rest of the passengers. They were in for a rough ride!

Chapter Ten

Nellie, her monkey, and the *Oriental* made it through the storm. The ship sailed into Hong Kong Bay the morning of December 23. It was two days ahead of schedule! In fact, the ship made it from Colombo to Hong Kong in record time.

Nellie stepped off the boat. She sat in a chair that was hoisted up on poles and carried by a driver. She was happy. It had been thirty-nine days since she left New York and she was now in China. Her driver left her at the steamship office.

"Will you tell me the date of the first sailing for Japan?" she asked at the desk.

"In one moment," the clerk said. He slipped off

into an office and came back with another man.

Nellie asked again about the next voyage to Japan.

"What is your name?" asked the other man.

"Nellie Bly," she said.

"Come in, come in," he answered nervously.

After Nellie was seated, he said, "You are going to be beaten."

Nellie answered, "What? I think not. I have made up my delay."

"You are going to lose it," he said.

"Lose it? I don't understand. What do you mean?" Nellie demanded. She was still not aware that anyone was racing against her.

"Aren't you having a race around the world?" he asked.

Nellie was confused. Of course she was. This made no sense to her.

"Yes, quite right. I am running a race with Time," she said.

"Time? I don't think that's her name," he said.

"Her! Her!" she repeated. This man was crazy.

"Yes, the other woman; she is going to win. She left here three days ago."

Nellie stared at him. "The other woman?" she asked.

The man then told her about the other woman who had left New York to race around the world against Nellie. She had already reached Hong Kong. Even worse, she had an editor who had paid extra money to keep her on schedule.

A sense of panic rose in Nellie. Her editor had said nothing about this other woman. Did the *World* know about her?

Then she heard the worse news. There was another delay. The ship that would take her to Japan would not be able to leave Hong Kong for five days!

An officer from the ship came in and tried to calm her. "You must not mind about the possibility of someone getting around the world in less time than you may do it.... Whether you get in before or later, people will give you the credit of having originated the idea."

"I promised my editor that I would go around the world in seventy-five days, and if I accomplish that, I shall be satisfied," Nellie answered. "I am not racing with anyone. I would not race. If someone else wants to do the trip in less time, that is their concern. If they take it upon themselves to race *against* me, it is their lookout that they succeed. I am not racing. I promised to do the trip in seventy-five days, and I will do it."

Nellie left the office for her hotel determined to win. Back in New York, the *World* was also ignoring Elizabeth's journey. Its readers were excitedly following Nellie's adventure every step of the way. Her race was only half over. There was one ocean and one continent left to cross. Nellie knew she could do it!

Chapter Eleven

Nellie spent five days in Hong Kong, waiting impatiently for the *Oceanic* to leave for Japan. People asked her to join them at dinner, but that didn't make her feel better. Since she had just one dress, she only went to dinners and events held in her honor. It was hard not to accept other invitations. She did, however, manage to see a play called *Ali Baba and the Forty Thieves*.

She watched the well-dressed women arrive at the theater. They did not travel in horse-drawn carriages. They were carried in on chairs lifted on poles, like in Singapore. In Hong Kong, the chairs were dressed with silk hangings and held on silver poles. They were so cheap that some

women owned multiple chairs. Many chairs even had cloth hangings that closed around them. This gave women privacy as they were carried along public streets. Some men had chairs, too. They were open chairs made of bent willow twigs.

As Nellie got ready to set sail again, she met the captain. She expected an old man with a well-worn face. Instead she found a young man with very blue eyes. She couldn't help laughing when she met him.

"You were so different to what I imagined you would be," she later said.

"And I could not believe you were the right girl, you were so unlike what I had been led to believe," said the captain. "I was told that you were an old maid with a dreadful temper."

They both were very happy to find they had been wrong.

Since Nellie had days to wait, she decided to see more of the country. She bought passage on

the *Powan*. It was a steamship that was traveling up the Pearl River from Hong Kong to Canton.

Back home, the *World* readers wondered how Nellie would spend Christmas Day. The paper said that Christmas Day for Nellie would be "an interesting and merry one, no doubt." There were many English speakers in Hong Kong, and some celebrated Christmas. Surely it would be a friendly holiday. But Nellie was not having a splendid holiday feast there. She was traveling with a group in the city of Canton. They were far from anyone who was celebrating the holiday.

Nellie was so happy to see the American flag flying over the American consulate on Christmas Day. It was the first time she'd seen one since she left New York. Nellie felt as if she was with an old friend.

"That is the most beautiful flag in the world, and I am ready to whip anyone who says it isn't," she said. And Nellie meant it. Her fellow travelers were afraid to say a single word.

Nellie had heard harsh things about the city of Canton. She was told that women there usually spat in the faces of female tourists. She had heard men might even toss a stone at her. These rumors weren't true. People did rush out of shops to see her. She wore odd American clothes that they had never seen. Some were even bold enough to come and touch her gloves.

The day finally arrived for Nellie to set sail on the *Oceanic*. The ship was splendid. The crew did everything to make the trip comfortable and pleasant for everyone aboard. The first thing Nellie did on the ship was to ask a stewardess how her monkey was.

"We have met," the stewardess said. The woman's arm was bandaged from her wrist to her shoulder. Nellie was alarmed.

"What did you do?" Nellie asked.

"I did nothing but scream; the monkey did the rest!" she replied.

Nellie still hadn't named her monkey. When she boarded, she decided on McGinty.

The ship sailed on during the last day of the year. On New Year's Eve, everyone aboard had a party with games and songs. Before Nellie knew it, she was in Japan at the Grand Hotel. Like the other stops, she would stay put while the ship got ready to sail again. It meant 120 hours in Japan.

Nellie enjoyed them all.

Japan was beautiful, and the people were kind. She called it Eden. She later said that she would even consider leaving her beloved America to go back. She thought it was the land of love, beauty, poetry, and cleanliness. She loved the Japanese custom of honoring the new year. People decorated doors with rice trimmings mixed with seaweed, orange, lobster, and ferns,

for good luck. She watched geisha girls with gold and silver flowers in their hair, dressed in beautiful kimonos. She said, "It would fill a large book if I attempted to describe all I saw during my stay in Japan."

She had only one regret. When she left New York, she had forgotten to pack a camera.

Chapter Twelve

It was a bright Tuesday morning on January 7 when Nellie left Japan. She enjoyed her visit but was eager to take her final voyage. She hoped for a quick sail to San Francisco. This was Nellie's last sailing and the crew was excited for her. They were so eager for her success that they wrote a poem in the engine room:

For Nellie Bly,
We'll win or die.

January 20, 1889

The trip began well, but on the fourth day the weather became very bad. Heavy rains and strong winds slammed the ship. Would it keep Nellie from breaking Phileas Fogg's pace? No one knew.

Nellie feared that she would arrive at the *World*'s offices too late. She would be the famous loser of a famous race.

"If I fail, I will never return to New York," she told the ship's officers.

The crew did everything to keep Nellie's hopes up, but it grew very hard as the storm continued for over four days.

Nellie was beginning to get superstitious. Cats and ministers on a ship were believed to be unlucky. Perhaps her monkey was unlucky? Some of the sailors thought so. Nellie hoped not.

Nellie had become swept up in the race during her trip. There were so many connections

to make and delays to be worked out. It became hard to think of anything else, even reporting. She had kept up a fast pace for months. Now she was at the mercy of the sea. She asked the ship's engineer to make the ship go faster.

On January 18 at 10:00 a.m., Elizabeth's train chugged into the station at Calais. She was also nearing the end of her journey. Who would arrive in New York first?

Nellie was just days away from reaching the United States. On January 21, the *Oceanic* sailed into San Francisco Bay—a day ahead of schedule! She was almost home!

But instead of feeling the joy she should have felt, she was hit with a big problem. The purser, or money handler, on the ship told Nellie some bad news. The bill of health was left behind in Japan. Nellie asked what that meant.

"It means that no one will be permitted to land until the next ship arrives from Japan. That will be two weeks," he said.

Nellie's heart sunk. How could that be? She was so close. She could see San Francisco. Her goal was just in reach.

Could he be wrong? Maybe it was just lost? The purser left to look one more time. Nellie held her breath. When he came back with it in his hand, Nellie was overjoyed.

Nellie was all set to leave the ship when more bad news came. It was the largest snow blockade in the history of the United States. Drifts of snow in the mountains of California had reached twenty feet high. Train travel through the west was shut down. Even though she could now leave the ship, how would she get to New York?

Chapter Thirteen

Readers of the *World* held their breath again when they read the bad news:

NELLIE BLY MAY BE DELAYED
AFTER LEAVING
SAN FRANCISCO

Nellie had gone more than 18,000 miles. So far she had stayed on time. But winter weather in the United States was a problem. This was why Elizabeth's editor sent her in the opposite direction. The trip across the United States might just change the outcome of the race.

Up until this point Nellie had not taken any special ships or trains. Now the *World* stepped in. They arranged for a special train to carry Nellie from Oakland, California, to Chicago, Illinois. The train would travel south of the snow. Messages were set along the route. The trains were to use the fastest engines for Nellie's trip.

The railroad charged the *World* a dollar a mile for the special service. The total cost came to $2,190. That was more than the cost of the entire rest of her trip.

She stepped onto the train. She had almost 3,000 miles left. Crowds greeted her at every stop along the way. Bands played. All of America cheered for her return. The four and a half days spent crossing the country were a blur.

"I only remember my trip across the continent as one maze of happy greetings, happy wishes, congratulating telegrams, fruit, flowers, loud cheers, wild hurrahs, rapid handshaking, and a beautiful car filled with fragrant flowers attached to a swift engine that was tearing

like mad through flower-dotted valley and over snow-tipped mountain, on—on—on! It was glorious!" she said.

As she got closer the crowds grew bigger. People came from far and wide to see Nellie. She was the American woman who had traveled all the way around the world.

Carriages waited for her in Chicago. There she was carried off to the Press Club to celebrate with her fellow journalists. But the party couldn't last too long. Nellie needed to get to New York!

When she boarded the train bound for New York, she was handed a very special note. It came from Jules Verne. He wanted to congratulate her on the moment her foot touched American soil. She had done it! Nellie Bly had gone completely around the world, and she was nearing home.

These were the last days of her trip. The *World* and its readers were just as excited. A small train was pictured on the front page of the paper. It showed how far she had come and how far she had left. Each day it inched closer to New York.

Nellie stopped in Philadelphia and gave a speech. Then a few of her friends joined her for her very last train ride. She was nearing Jersey City, where she had boarded her first ship months before.

The train sped to the station. It slowed to a

stop. Nellie had traveled around the entire world. She jumped out onto the platform. A cheer went up from the crowd. Nellie waved her now-famous cap. She wanted to cheer along with everyone else. But it wasn't because she had finished her trip in seventy-two days. Or because she had beaten Phileas Fogg. She wanted to cheer because she was now home!

Afterword

Nellie Bly began her trip on November 14, 1889. She returned to New York on January 25, 1890. She finished her trip in record time. She beat both Phileas Fogg and Elizabeth Bisland.

A man named F. W. Stevens won the *World*'s Guessing Match game. He guessed within fifteen seconds of Nellie's arrival. The *World* spared no time in writing up Nellie's adventures. Someone drew a cartoon of Nellie in a row of male adventurers. SHE'S BROKEN EVERY RECORD, the title read. The paper printed a game for people to play. It was called ROUND THE WORLD WITH NELLIE BLY. They even gave away photos of Nellie to people who bought a paper.

Nellie had become one of the best reporters of her time. She knew how to choose a story topic. She also knew how to put herself into the center of her stories. People wanted to read more by Nellie Bly. It made her even more famous. Soon she was off for a forty-city tour, like a rock star!

Her record-breaking trip put her in the history books. She was only twenty-five years old and the most famous woman on the planet. Nellie Bly caps became a fashion hit. A hotel, a race horse, and a train were named after her. Nellie's face was even painted on serving plates.

Elizabeth Bisland also beat Phileas Fogg's pace. She arrived four days after Nellie. She left for England not long after. She didn't want to be in the headlines.

After Nellie's tour ended, she continued to cover important stories for the *World*. Later she became the first woman journalist on the Eastern Front during World War I.

THE STORY BEHIND THE STORY

THE RACE AROUND THE WORLD

COMMUNICATION

Nellie couldn't send an email or make a cell phone call on her journey. Email and cell phones didn't exist. She had to send messages by telegraph. A cable under the ocean  carried messages to the United States. Nellie had to find a telegraph office each time she wanted to send a message. Her more detailed notes were written by hand and sent by ship. They took much longer to arrive.

FAMOUS WRITERS

Nellie Bly was one of many famous writers in the United States. Everyone knew Mark Twain's characters Huckleberry Finn and Tom Sawyer. Twain's books were published just a few years before Nellie's trip. Louisa May Alcott wrote a famous book called *Little Women*. Many authors from Europe were popular, including Charles Dickens. He had toured the United States twice before Nellie's famous trip.

THE LATE LOUISA MAY ALCOTT.—From a Photograph.—[See Page 257.]

WOMEN HEROES

Who were the other women making news in America? Sharpshooter Annie Oakley was a legend when Nellie was alive. She starred in Buffalo Bill's Wild West Show. Jane Addams was a social reformer. She was well known for helping people. She earned the 1931 Nobel Peace Prize. Grandma Moses's folk art was on the way to becoming famous. Helen Keller was ten years old when Nellie returned from her trip. Many women, like Lucy Stone, Susan B. Anthony, and Frances Elizabeth Willard, were making news fighting for women's right to vote.

Nicknames

The *World* had lots of fun names for Nellie in their pages. Here are a few:

A Veritable Feminist Phileas Fogg

The *World*'s Feminine Mercury

The *World*'s Plucky Globetrotter

Our Little Globe-Girdler

The *World*'s Globe-Circler

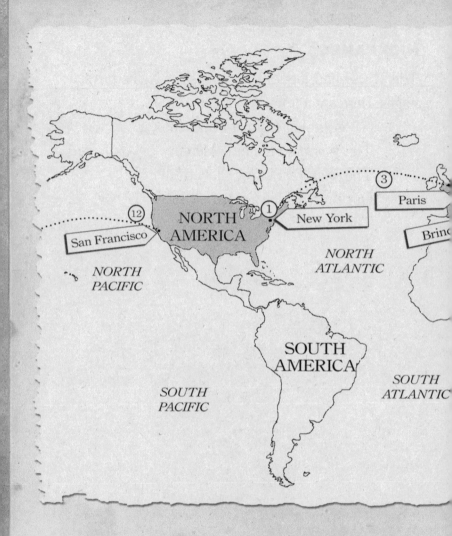

Countries Nellie Visited:
England, France, Italy, Egypt, Japan,
and the United States

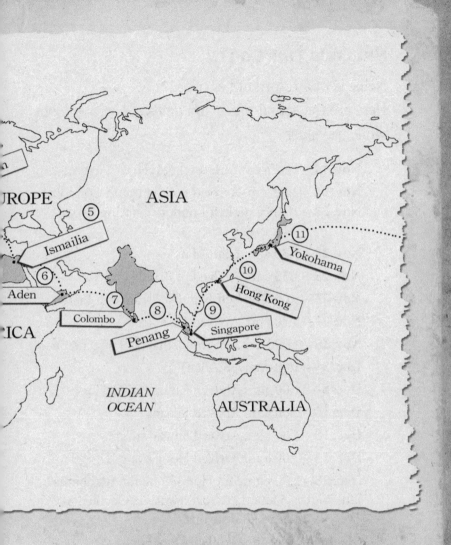

British Possessions Nellie Visited:
Aden, Arabia; Colombo, Isle of Ceylon; Penang,
Prince of Wales Island; Singapore, Malay Peninsula;
and the island of Hong Kong

NELLIE'S TRIP LOG

Nellie kept a record of her trips.
Here are the actual times and dates she wrote down while traveling:

Nov. 14—Left New York on the *Augusta Victoria*

Nov. 22—2:30 a.m. Arrived Southampton-London

Nov. 22—10:00 a.m. Left London, Charing Cross Station

Nov. 23—1:30 a.m. Left Calais

Nov. 25—1:30 a.m. Arrived in Brindisi

Nov. 25—3:00 a.m. Left Brindisi, steamship *Victoria*

Nov. 27—3:30 p.m. Arrived Port Said

Nov. 28—11:00 a.m. Arrived Ismallia, 9:00 p.m. Suez

Dec. 3—11:00 Arrived Aden

Dec. 8—11:00 a.m. Arrived Colombo (Ceylon)

Dec. 16—7:00 a.m. Arrived Penang

Dec. 18—5:00 a.m. Arrived Singapore

Dec. 25—7:00 a.m. Arrived Hong Kong

Dec. 28—2:30 p.m. Left Hong Kong for Yokohama

Jan. 7—10:55 a.m. Left Yokohama via Occidental and Oriental steamship

Jan. 21—8:00 a.m. Arrived in San Francisco

Jan. 23—7:05 a.m. Arrived Chicago

Jan. 25—3:51 p.m. Arrived New York

NELLIE'S WORLD RECORD

November 14–January 25:
72 days

Nellie's total time:
1,734 hours, 11 minutes
or
72 days, 6 hours, 11 minutes

Nellie's average speed on her journey
(including stops):
28.71 miles per hour

FURTHER RESOURCES

Here are a few more nonfiction resources about Nellie Bly:

BOOKS

- Blos, Joan W., illustrated by Catherine Stock. *Nellie Bly's Monkey.* New York: HarperCollins, 1996.
- Bly, Nellie. *Nellie Bly's Book: Around the World in Seventy-Two Days.* New York: Pictorial Weekly, 1890.
- Macy, Sue. *Bylines: A Photobiography of Nellie Bly.* New York: National Geographic Children's Books, 2009.

MOVIES AND TELEVISION

- *The Adventures of Nellie Bly.* Dir. Henning Schellerup. Perf. Linda Purl. Schick Sunn Classics, 1981.
- "Around the World in 72 Days." Dir. Christine Lesiak. Perf. David Ogden Stiers. *The American Experience*/WGBH Educational Foundation, 1997. PBS.
- *Around the World in 80 Days.* Dir. Frank Coraci. Perf. Jackie Chan and Steve Coogan. Walt Disney Pictures, 2004.

WEBSITES

- Nellie Bly Online: nellieblyonline.com
- National Women's History Museum and Girls Learn International: nwhm.org/online-exhibits /youngandbrave/bly.html

PLACES TO VISIT

- DiMenna Children's History Museum: See the Game of Round the World with Nellie Bly (New York).
- National Women's Hall of Fame: Check out more on Nellie and other female journalists (Seneca Falls, NY).
- Newseum: See Nellie's bag and board game. Watch a 4-D movie featuring Nellie (Washington, D.C.).

PLAN A TRIP

Plan your own trip around the world. It's easy today to travel the world in eighty days. You just have to purchase a round-the-world (RTW) airline ticket. With an RTW, you must pick a direction—and stick to it. Would you go east like Nellie Bly or west like Elizabeth Bisland? Where would you like to visit? What would you like to see? What would you pack?

Try your hand at creating a map of the places you would visit if you had the chance to fly around the world in eighty days. Check out lonelyplanet.com/travel-tips-and-articles/77749 for tips.

About the Author

NANCY CASTALDO loves to write books for curious readers and also enjoys traveling (perhaps as much as Nellie!). She's traveled to many places to research her books, including Russia! Once she even traveled for three weeks in Norway and Italy with just a backpack and one pair of shoes—not exactly one dress or seventy-two days, but a challenge nonetheless!

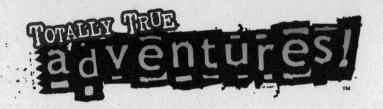

CLIMBING EVEREST

Crack! An edge of ice split off and dropped into the deep dark hole. Hillary fell. He tried to slow himself by jamming his boots into the icy wall.

"Tenzing!" he shouted. "Tenzing!"

In a flash, Tenzing plunged his ice ax into the snow. He wrapped his rope around the ax to hold it steady. Then he threw himself on the ground, to anchor the rope even more.

The rope tightened. Hillary jerked to a stop. He was fifteen feet down, far into the crack of ice. Bit by bit, he pulled himself up. His gloves were torn, and his body was bruised. But he was alive.

Excerpt copyright © 2015 by Gail Herman. Published by Random House Children's Books, a division of Penguin Random House LLC, New York.